CONTENTS

GENERAL LEARNING OBJECTIVES OF THIS UNIT

This Open Learning Unit will introduce you to the principles of the scientific method and its application in the Behavioural and Social Sciences. It provides the background needed for designing investigations using a broad range of methods and explains the particular advantages of each approach. It provides the factual information and explains the fundamental principles that are needed to answer examination questions on research methods and to design your own research projects effectively. It provides essential background for the Units on *Describing and Interpreting Data* (Unit 2) and on *Drawing Inferences from Statistical Data* (Unit 3).

By the end of this Unit, you should understand:

> how to formulate precise research questions;

> how scientific models are used for explanation and prediction;

> the need for several different methods of investigation;

> the importance – and the difficulty – of distinguishing among multiple possible causes for results that are observed.

Asking answerable questions

KEY AIMS: By the end of Part 1 you should understand:
▷   *how to ask scientific questions that have answers;*
▷   *the need to be precise about what is to be measured;*
▷   *the difference between absolute and relative descriptions;*
▷   *three types of scientific conclusion.*

Victoria: Blokko chocolate is best.
Albert: Frothibars are nicer. They're bigger too.
Victoria: No they're not. Look. Your Frothibar is 100 g and my Blokko's 125 g
Albert: That just means it's heavier; Frothibar is much thicker.

SOMETHING TO TRY
Below is a list of possible points of dispute between Victoria and Albert.
> *Which bar is heavier?*
> *Which bar is longer?*
> *Which bar is thicker?*
> *Which bar is wider?*
> *Which bar is bigger?*
> *Which bar is cheaper?*
> *Which bar tastes nicer?*
> *Which bar is best?*

Before reading further, consider which points they might be able to agree on after examining both bars of chocolate.

Which bar is heavier? Some disagreements can be settled on the basis of suitable evidence that convinces anyone that one particular answer is correct. For instance, everyone should agree about which is *heavier, longer, thicker* and *wider* since we all know reliable ways of measuring these things and all Blokkos are the same (or very nearly so) and so are Frothibars .

Which bar is bigger? There is likely to be some problem in reaching agreement about the other descriptions. The meaning of 'bigger', for instance, isn't very exact. Victoria interprets it as *heavier* while Albert thinks it means *thicker.* They might agree to apply it to the bar with the greatest volume, but then again they might not.

Which bar is cheaper? Cheapness is easy to measure, but the problem is that shops sell chocolate at different prices so there may be a different answer for each shop. Since there is no single, correct answer we might settle for an answer that is *usually* right and compare their average prices. Alternatively, we may try to decide which type of bar is *most often* sold at the lower price.

Which bar tastes nicer? People are likely to agree about which of two foods is the *sweeter*, if the difference isn't too small, but they are much less likely to agree about which tastes *nicer.* Some prefer sweeter chocolate than others, some like it dark and others like it milky. People are not wrong to have these different preferences, but it means that there is no correct answer to agree about – nothing that can be measured to settle the argument. As with cheap-

1

ness, we might settle for an answer that isn't true in every case but applies to most people, such as investigating whether more people select Blokko or Frothibar when given a free choice.

Which bar is best? The problem about deciding which is *best* is similar, only worse, because now as well as having to consider how much we like the taste we also have to consider whether we think it's good value for money, whether it's the right size to eat all at once, and so on. All these aspects are difficult to measure. Also, people may not agree about their relative importance. One person may think taste is more important than value for money and someone else might think the opposite.

Helen Welford

A word of warning
Although we use terms like the 'nicest taste' or the 'best chocolate', we must not forget that *niceness* and *goodness* are not *properties of the chocolate*. They are descriptions of how we feel about chocolate, and each person may have different feelings. If you ask two people which of two pictures is more beautiful and they give different answers, is one of them wrong? No! They are not telling you something about the pictures but about themselves and what they like, and they are entitled to like different things. Any time a term refers to human feelings and preferences, we may find people giving different answers which are equally correct.

Absolutes and relatives

Apart from the problem of exactly what measurements are relevant, there is always some uncertainty when a quantitative term – *large, tiny, fast* – is used on its own to describe a single item ('the car travels fast'). Quantitative terms used in this way are **absolute**; whereas when they are used to compare two or more things they become **relative**, and their meaning is much clearer ('the car travels faster than the bicycle').

Is a rabbit a *large* animal? Not if you compare it to humans or to elephants, but considered beside all the animal species on earth, it's well into the top 1% in terms of size. When using quantitative terms, it's best to use them as relative terms: 'rabbits are larger than mice'.

Helen Welford

Types of conclusion

If all the members of a group (all Blokkos, say) are alike, then studying one of them tells you about all of them. Of course you would usually need to study more than one to satisfy yourself that indeed they *are* all alike! Blokkos have the same weight, length and so on, so it's easy to decide whether Blokkos or Frothibars are heavier or longer because the answer is always the same. Answers to scientific questions that are true in every individual case are called **general conclusions**.

Blokkos are not sold *at the same price* everywhere, so we can't decide whether Blokkos or Frothibars are cheaper by studying only one of each. Scientific conclusions that are only *mostly* true are called **aggregate conclusions.** When our question concerns living things, we can almost never assume that individuals of the same kind are alike so we can only reach aggregate conclusions about them. The consequences are that in psychology:

- we almost always have to study several individuals;
- we usually reach conclusions that are only *mostly* true.

It's very important to understand whether a scientific conclusion is aggregate or general, because if we overlook the distinction we may make mistakes in the deductions we draw. For example, if we discover in a survey of many shops that Blokkos are, on average, cheaper than Frothibars (that is an *aggregate* conclusion) we would be wrong to deduce that Victoria's Blokko must have cost less than Albert's Frothibar. She may have bought it in an expensive shop.

Occasionally it may be useful to reach a weaker kind of conclusion that is neither of these types, called an **existential conclusion**. It merely states that something *exists* or that something *can happen*, without implying that it always, or even usually, happens. Suppose we find that, in cars fitted with a particular design of speedometer, drivers make a type of error that never occurs with other speedometer designs. That conclusion may be important even if the errors occur only rarely.

Some examples

For each of the numbered questions:

➤   Will the answer be an aggregate or a general statement?

➤   Would everyone agree about whether it's true or false?

➤   What sort of evidence would persuade someone who disagrees?

➤   If there is no single, correct answer, modify the question so that there is one. (We will then have something specific to measure.)

1. *Can boys run faster than girls?*
2. *Is French easier than German?*
3. *Is Maths difficult?*
4. *Do happy people work harder than miserable ones?*

Answers

All of the questions are phrased in a way that appears to expect a general conclusion, applying to every individual concerned, but *none* of these questions has an answer that is guaranteed to be correct for everyone. For that reason you can not be sure of persuading others to accept an answer to any of the questions, whatever evidence you provide. People may, however, be willing to agree to aggregate conclusions about the same topics.

If we interpret the questions as aggregate, it would be better to express them differently. We can change a question to make it one that everyone interprets in the same way and also to make it clear that the answer is not expected to apply in every single case. Then we should be able to seek persuasive evidence, remembering that we may be answering a *different* question from the one we began with. We will consider each question in turn.

▷   1. *Can boys run faster than girls?* Some boys can run faster than some girls but some girls can run faster than some boys. Also, individual boys and girls run faster at some times than at others. If we organize a race with several boys and several girls in it, we could see whether the boys or the girls tend to do better (There are many other matters that we ought to take account of, though, such as their ages.) More precise questions are:
Do most boys run faster than most girls?
Is the average running speed of boys higher than that of girls?

▷   2. *Is French easier than German?* Obviously people in France and Germany would have different answers and so would anyone who studied one of the languages and not the other. Even if learning starts from the same point, the answer might be different depending on whether we mean writing, reading, speaking or listening to the language. One language might be easier for learning a few phrases but be the more difficult one for acquiring fluency, and so on. One out of many possible questions would be:
In which language do English pupils learning both languages at the same time know more words at the end of one year of study?

▷   3. *Is Maths difficult?* There is probably nobody who does not consider *some form* of maths difficult, but any given problem may be considered easy by some and difficult by others, so the word *maths* is too vague to be useful. If, instead, we ask about a particular kind of maths, or even a particular maths problem, we still haven't made the question answerable. Unless we can attach a specific meaning to the word *difficult* there is no answer. The word is an example of an absolute quantitative term. Note that in the previous example, we considered whether one language was more difficult than another. Comparing two or more difficulties is much easier. Possible questions would be:
Do university students of mathematics more often fail examinations in geometry or in algebra?
What proportion of the adult population can solve the equation: $x = 5x - 8$?

Helen Welford

▷ 4. Do *happy people work harder than miserable ones*? The words *happy* and *miserable* cause problems if we regard them as absolute quantities, but the problems are greatly reduced if we interpret them as comparative terms; that is, if we divide people into those who are nearer to being *happy* and those who are nearer to being *miserable*, without having to ensure that anyone is exactly one or the other. The term 'work harder' isn't very precise either. Does it mean *work longer hours, try harder, achieve more*, or what? A possible question would be:

Do those who are rated by their workmates as being above average in happiness miss fewer days from work than those rated below average in happiness?

(Note that even when we learn the answer we still do not know if they miss working days because they are unhappy or are unhappy because they miss working days, or perhaps neither of these.)

Summary

If evidence is to convince everyone that a statement is true, we need:
> (a) agreement about *exactly* what property is described by the statement;
> (b) agreement about how to measure it.

If we fail to get agreement on these two conditions, some people are likely to remain unconvinced.

SAQ
1

(a) *Are these conclusions aggregate or general?*
> *Adult rabbits are heavier than adult mice.*
> *Ten-year-old children know more words than eight-year-olds.*

(b) *For each of the examples, invent a conclusion of the other kind about the same topic.*

Models to explain observations

Albert: Jane's scowling at me.
Victoria: Oh it's not just you. She's upset with everyone.
Albert: No, I think it's me she's angry with. She crossed the room to avoid sitting near me.
Victoria: I think she wanted to be near the window. She doesn't feel very good today.

It seems that Albert and Victoria have different ideas about why Jane is behaving the way she is. They agree about what Jane has *done* but have different explanations. They can't be certain of their explanations, but they will each behave in a way that reflects the ideas they have formed about *why* she is acting as she is. Victoria will try to comfort her while Albert will probably avoid her or might confront her. Both would be acting on the basis of a mental **model**. Albert's model has Jane being angry with him personally. Victoria's model has Jane feeling unwell and upset, but not particularly angry with anyone. The advantage of models is that they allow us to predict the reactions of the other person in many related situations, not only to Jane at this particular time and place. The model includes general information about how 'angry people', or 'people who feel unwell', react to events around them. This means that we can anticipate how Jane will respond to being ignored, or confronted, or comforted. But of course the two models make different predictions; only if the model is accurate will the predictions be correct. If they watch Jane more closely, or make some friendly approach to her that does not depend too much on either model they might gain enough extra information from her reactions to decide in favour of one or the other. Another possibility is that the information they gain will allow them to adjust or adapt one of the models to fit the facts better.

Any time we feel we *understand* what is happening, it is because we *have a model*. Having a model lets us go beyond what we are experiencing at the moment to make predictions of what will happen in the future or under different circumstances.

Laws of nature are models

Most of science is concerned with developing and testing models. Practically anything that you think of as a scientific fact or a law of nature is really just a successful model. For instance, you can not experience gravity, though you can experience things that nowadays we attribute to the effects of gravity, such as objects falling to the ground. But it is not obvious that you need to invoke an invisible force that acts without contact to explain this. Indeed, for most of human history people managed perfectly well without the idea. What made gravity a very appealing model was that it explained such a lot. It explained not only why apples fall but also why the sun rises, why tides rise and fall, why stars and planets move in different ways and why comets appear in the sky on rare occasions. Before Newton, people had separate models for all these phenomena but his model explained them all. However, we now know that Newton's model of gravity does not always work exactly, and new models that include it as a special case have replaced it.

"He doesn't understand gravity yet"

Devising and testing models

That is how science goes. By constructing models we gain understanding; the models let us make predictions; we test the predictions and if they are fulfilled we make further predictions, and so on. But, eventually, it often happens that even a very successful model turns out not to be exactly correct in every possible situation. When that happens, someone has to invent a new model. Psychology (and the behavioural sciences in general) works like that too, both the informal kind of psychology Albert and Victoria were discussing and research that is done in laboratories.

Discovering laws

In fact, there are two functions of models that need to be distinguished, though they overlap a good deal. One is *making predictions* and the other is *gaining understanding*. An example will illustrate the distinction.

SOMETHING TO TRY

In the land of Ozzipan there is a law that all new houses must be numbered, and anyone who gives a house an illegal number will be punished. But they are very secretive about what numbers you are allowed to use. You have just built a new house and the numbers running along your street are: 1 2 3 4 5 6 7 ? Your house is the question mark. What number will you give it?

Assuming the number you pick is acceptable, if somebody now comes and builds next to your house, what number would you expect the newcomer to choose?

STT Answer

You would have been okay to number your house 8, and in the circumstances that is what most people would do. If your new neighbour uses the number 9, that too will be legal. You probably used the simple numerical model: add one to the number next door. It happens to satisfy the Ozzipandians, even though it is not, in fact, their law.

The actual law is: *all the numbers in a street must be different.*

Seeking data to contradict a model

If your purpose had been to discover *what the law is* rather than to make a successful prediction, you might not have chosen 8. It would have been interesting to try some other number to see if the sequence could be broken. Certainly, if you were able to allocate several numbers and were trying to find the exact form of the law it would be a bad plan to keep on making only successful predictions by always using the same model. Instead, you should try out various models. If they make wrong predictions you reject them. But if one of them makes a prediction that turns out to be legal though the simple, numerical model said it wasn't, then the earlier model must be discarded. You would soon discover that it wasn't necessary to add one every time. You would be allowed to add any number, or even to subtract, as long as that didn't cause you to repeat an earlier number.

We should never be satisfied with a model if we only have results that the model predicts. We must also show that the model correctly predicts which results *will not* occur. Even though it never makes wrong predictions of *what will be allowed*, the model of adding one every time is wrong because it predicts that it would be illegal to add three or seventeen and it isn't.

Models that can not be rejected are bad!

It might seem that an ideal model is one that can explain absolutely anything that happens; but that is the very opposite of the truth. If it can always explain whatever occurs, a model can not be proved wrong and is said to be **unfalsifiable**. That too might seem like an advantage, but it is not so.

A model is impossible to prove wrong only if it can account for absolutely anything that occurs. If that is true, it follows that there can be nothing that the model says *must not* happen and there can be nothing that it says *must* happen. It is a very severe criticism of any scientific model to say that it is unfalsifiable because any such model is unable to make any definite predictions. It can give explanations but not predictions; and because its explanation must happen *after* the event that is explained, it can really be no more than a translation of what was observed into a description in different words.

Summary

If we want to *understand* what living things experience, what they do and why they do it, we must speculate about possible models and then collect data to see which models can be supported by evidence and which must be rejected. We hope to end up with good models that correctly predict both the things that do happen and those that do not. A model may be rejected because it says that something *must not* occur, but it does occur, or because it says something *must* occur but it does not. But in order to do that, we must be able to make predictions from it and we must be able to say if the results we obtain do or do not agree with them. That is not as easy as it might seem. This Unit is mainly about ways of collecting data and of interpreting it to see which models it agrees with.

SAQ
2

Explain why scientific results can prove that a model is wrong but can never prove that it is correct.

Models for measurement

KEY AIMS: By the end of Part 3 you should understand:
▷   *that measurement means using numbers as an abstract model for real things;*
▷   *that properties of the measurement model determine how numbers can be used;*
▷   *that there are different levels of measurement;*
▷   *the properties of the scale types, nominal, ordinal, interval and ratio.*

Albert: Frothibars are ten times as good as Blokkos.
Victoria: Okay, here's a good bargain: I'll give you one Frothibar for five Blokkos!

Models to guide exploration

A model can be a sort of *guess about how things are*. You form models when trying to find your way out of a room you don't know in the dark. You encounter a hard, vertical surface and have to decide how to treat it. If it's a wall of the room it will pay to feel your way along it until you come to a door, but if it's a wardrobe, that will not be a good plan!

The 'wall' model and the 'wardrobe' model can be tested. Probably, the sound made when you knock on the surface will be different in each case; probably, the texture or the warmth of the surface will be different, and so on. Such evidence is not absolutely guaranteed to tell you which is correct, but they will indicate which is more believable. You then plan your further actions accordingly. As you explore further, you get extra information that makes you more and more sure which model is the correct one. Each time you encounter a new object, you have to create further models to explain it. Is it a table or a chair? Is it a bed or a sofa? Is it a rug or a sleeping cat? As you explore, you also build up a model of the whole room. Is it a bedroom or a kitchen? Is it square or long and narrow? Is it full of furniture or fairly bare? In this way you both *make predictions* and *gain understanding*. By the time you have a lot of information, you will be pretty sure your model is a good one that can safely be relied on for deciding what to do. Models that don't agree with the evidence will have been discarded.

Models as simplification

The key characteristic of a model is that it is *simpler* than the thing it represents. In feeling your way through the room, you don't care what colour the wall is painted, nor what kind of wood the wardrobe is made of, nor whether it's glued, nailed or bolted together, so these properties are not part of your model. The real objects have unlimited numbers of properties, which you needn't bother about while you solve the immediate problem of finding a way out. To that extent, the models you use are abstract, because they represent only certain properties that matter to you at the moment.

Models to make calculation possible

A particularly useful model for properties of the world is provided by *numbers*. A model using numbers is completely abstract and is always simpler than the things it represents.

The reason it pays to use numbers as a model is that we can use numbers to get useful answers. If I put two eggs in a basket and later put in another three, it seems obvious that the basket now holds enough to give one each to five people. But that is obvious to you only because some calculations are so familiar that we do them without effort. We have left aside the idea of actual *eggs* and focused on the *abstract* idea of 2 + 3 = 5. That is, we have represented real objects (eggs) by a **numerical model** and then carried out arithmetic on the numbers.

Numerical problems vary greatly in difficulty. It may be easy to calculate the number of eggs in a basket if we know how many we put in each time, but to calculate how many overlapping tiles are needed for a complex roof might defeat us. Yet a builder needs to do the calculation rather than order too many or too few. There are even more complex problems that engineers have to solve. How thick must a certain beam be to support a bridge? How wide must the base of a dam be if it is to hold back the water safely? How much power must a ship's engines generate if it is to travel at 30 knots?

Calculation beats trial and error. One way to answer such questions is to try it and see. If our first attempt doesn't work, we try again, making the beam stronger, the dam thicker, the engines more powerful. But that is a very expensive and dangerous way to proceed. Instead, engineers work out the answers, not with the real-world objects they are constructing but with *abstract, numerical models*. That is, they use *numbers* to represent the relevant aspects of the objects and carry out calculations on these numbers. The way that numbers reflect properties of the objects is called a **measurement model** and the process of obtaining numbers to represent things in the real world is called **measurement**.

Numbers have many properties, as we shall see, but not all the properties of numbers may be needed in a particular model. Real objects have infinitely many properties, but again only a few of them are relevant to a particular problem, and the others play no part in the model. It matters what the beam and the dam are made of, but not what colour they are. It matters how heavy the ship's engines are – but not what metal they are made of. The measurement model expresses the relationship between those properties of the objects that we must take account of and the properties of numbers needed for the problem in hand. Before useful calculations can be carried out on the numbers obtained by measurement, we must take account of which properties of the numbers correspond to properties of the objects. Exactly the same applies when we use numbers to describe living things and their behaviour.

Scales as measuring instruments

When we talk of 'scales' we usually think in terms of kitchen scales, thermometers or rulers; that is, we have the concept of measuring something. But if we try to apply this idea to psychological variables like aggression, anxiety, intelligence or creativity we can't construct anything as convenient as a ruler nor can we measure the variables directly. Instead we have to use indirect methods such as asking questions about various topics or setting tasks to be performed. We then have to use a scoring key or follow some rule in order to convert these results into numbers. Although we may refer to these numbers as a 'scale' they constitute data of a very different kind: it is impossible with such data to say if one person's score of 4 describes exactly the same thing as another person's score of 4 on the same scale. And 4 of what? Using a ruler we would have no difficulty in stating that a measurement of 4 (whether in inches, metres or centimetres) was half a measurement of 8 and twice one of 2; and that no matter what was being measured, when it was measured, or by whom, it would remain the same.

The ruler gives us an external, objective standard. More importantly, we have a direct way of checking that intervals on the ruler are equal. For example, a rod that is 10 mm long will exactly span the distance from 10 mm to 20 mm, or from 13 mm to 23 mm, or from 37 mm to 47 mm. The numerical difference between these scale readings is always 10. Unfortunately, there is no equivalent way to check that a difference of 10 on a psychological scale always has the same meaning, as we shall see.

What is meant by a score of 4 out of 7, say, on a scale of aggression? Can we say that a person with a score of 6 on an anxiety scale is twice as anxious as a person who scored 3 on the same scale? Probably not. So, if we are going to make sense of behavioural data it is crucial to understand what is the relationship between the numbers we get and the thing being measured. That is what is meant by the 'level' (or 'type' or 'scale') of measurement.

The various types must be carefully distinguished since any data that you collect, or have to deal with, will fall into one or more of these categories, and this will set boundaries for interpreting your data. Five important types of scale are:

nominal scales, **ordinal** scales, **interval** scales, **ratio** scales and **absolute** scales.

They all have to do with relationships between the properties of numbers and properties of the things we measure, and in each case the relationship is different. Further types of scale exist but are rarely met except in specialized work.

Nominal scales

The nominal scale describes the simplest use of numbers, and provides the least information of all the scales. With this scale, there is no relationship at all between the size of a number and any attribute 'measured' by it. For instance, bus routes may be given numbers 1 to 20, but a No. 14 bus may not exceed a No. 7 bus in any way – and you would certainly not think of catching two No. 7s if you really wanted a No. 14! A nominal scale simply uses numbers as convenient labels – the bus routes might just as well have been labelled the 'blue route', the 'red route', and so on.

Helen Welford

All that you can tell from numbers on a nominal scale is whether two things are equivalent in some respect (because they have the same number) or are different (because they have different numbers). The number serves only as a label or name (hence 'nominal', from the Latin word for 'name'). We should not use these numbers for arithmetic any more than we would use colours for arithmetic – the answers would be meaningless. However, we can *count how often* each number occurs and use the resulting **frequencies** in calculations. Comparing the frequency of the No. 7 bus with that of the No. 14 bus is quite okay, just as it would be quite okay to compare the numbers of red ones and blue ones. As we shall see later, frequency of occurrence is measured on an *absolute* scale, even if the events being counted are identified by numbers which represent only a *nominal* scale.

Actually, nominal scales are mentioned mainly to alert you to the possibility that numbers may tell you nothing at all about any property of the thing they refer to. We do not usually consider such use of numbers to be 'measurement' in any ordinary sense of the word. Other examples of numbers that are used just to identify things are: postal district numbers, telephone numbers, the numbers on footballers, and participants in an experiment being labelled 1, 2, 3, and so on.

Ordinal (or rank-order) scales

Ordinal scales give us more information. If we have an ordinal scale, we know not only if something occurs but can also make use of the position of a score within its own particular group of scores. The order by size of the numbers reflects the order by size of whatever has been measured: so, if A has more than B of some property, then A is assigned a larger number than B.

Conversely, if C has a bigger number than D, then C has more of the property being measured.

But, what we still can't tell from an ordinal scale is what the actual differences between the individual scores mean. For example, hotels are graded with 1, 2, 3, 4 or 5 stars to indicate their degree of luxury. The more stars they have, the more comfortable, large and expensive they are likely to be, yet the difference between 1-star and 2-star hotels is unlikely to be equal in any objective sense to that between 4-star and 5-star hotels. And it would be meaningless to describe a 4-star hotel as twice as comfortable as a 2-star one.

Let's look at another example. If all bus stops are numbered outwards from the city centre, with more frequent stops clustered in the centre, the bus stop numbers form an ordinal scale of distance. We don't know if the distance between stop 8 and stop 9 is the same as the difference between stops 1 and 2. All we can be sure of is that stop 9 is further from the city centre than stop 8, though we don't know *how much* further because the distances between them vary.

It is rather common in the behavioural sciences to find oneself working with 'untrustworthy' data in the sense that one is not quite sure of the exact relationship between the score obtained from the research and the thing being measured, even when we are confident that larger scores show that there is more of it. When that happens, it can be convenient before doing statistical analyses to convert the ordinal scores into **ranks**, by arranging the raw scores in rank order of increasing size and numbering them in a continuous sequence. Working with these rank numbers can help to remind us that differences between raw scores cannot be taken at face value, though of course the rank numbers too cannot tell us by how much the measured items differ.

Note that in statistical ordering it is more usual to give the lowest rank (1) to the lowest score and the highest rank to the highest score. This is opposite to one's normal, everyday experience where to come first in something usually implies the highest score!

> **To summarize:**
> ❑ ordinal measurements tell us more than nominal 'measurements';
> ❑ the position (or rank order) of an ordinal score in a group of scores tells us the position of the measured item in the corresponding group of items;
> ❑ however, we can't assume that equal intervals between scores represent equal differences between items and therefore we can't make any use of the actual difference between two scores, only their relative ranking within the group.

In order to make meaningful use of the difference between actual scores we need at least an interval scale, which is described in the next section.

Interval scales

With *interval* scales we can make more use of the actual scores than we can with ordinal scores, and this gives us much more information.

But, in order to claim that the scale of measurement you are using is a true interval scale, you must be certain (or fairly certain) that equal intervals on the scale represent equal differences in the property being measured. The difference in weight between 10 and 20 grams is the same as that between 50 and 60 grams, but what can we say about the difference between two people's scores on a memory test where one recalls 10 words and the other recalls 20? We can say with certainty that one recalled twice as many words as the other, but if we want to use the number of words as an indicator of memory power, would we be justified in saying that person A had twice the memory power of person B? Or that recalling 20 words rather than 10 required twice the mental effort? Obviously not. It is likely that the first 10 were easy to remember and it got progressively harder to remember more; that is, we cannot be sure that the intervals in what we are trying to measure (memory power or mental effort) were the same. Again, it is vitally necessary to relate the numbers you obtain to the thing being measured.

Continuing the example of bus stops numbered outwards from the city centre, suppose there is a stretch, from stops 10 to 20, in which the stops *are* equally spaced. The numbers along that part of the route constitute an *interval* scale of distance from the city centre. We can correctly deduce that the distance between stops 11 and 14 is the same as that between 17 and 20 or between stops 13 and 16 because these differences are all 3. However, we can *not* deduce that stop 20 is twice as far from the city centre as stop 10. If the bus stops are closer together in the centre, the distance from the centre to 10 will be smaller than that from 10 to 20. Also, I have not said that the numbering in the centre begins at zero! It is much more likely to begin at 1, though it could begin at 5 or any other number. For all these reasons, we must not make use of ratios of the bus stop numbers.

Consider again the memory test. In order to claim that recalling 20 words required twice the mental effort of recalling 10, we would need to know:
(a)   that each word required the same mental effort, and
(b)   that someone who recalled no words (that is, had a score of zero) must have made no mental effort.
The first of these is unlikely and the second is clearly wrong. The importance of scores of zero to the information you can get from measurements will be discussed further in the next section.

> **To summarize:**
> ❑   interval scales tell us more than ordinal scales;
> ❑   with an interval scale, equal differences in numbers represent equal differences in the things measured;
> ❑   however, with an interval scale we cannot say that one measured item is twice or three times as great as another. For that, we require a *ratio* scale, described in the next section.

Ratio scales

You don't often need to worry about the difference between interval and ratio scales since for the purposes of statistical analysis they can usually be treated in the same way. But some conclusions (those involving ratios of scores) are meaningful only with a ratio scale.

Of the four types discussed so far, the ratio scale conveys the most information. On this scale, equal differences in number denote equal differences in the measured variable, just as in the interval scale and, in addition, the number zero denotes complete absence of the attribute being measured. Because of that extra property, it now makes sense not only to speak of differences being equal but also to speak of one measurement being twice or three times another. That was not true for any of the other scales.

Most of the measurements we make in daily life, for example of weight or of distance, are made on ratio scales, but true ratio scales for psychological variables are very rare. However, people are often willing to *assume* that measurement is on an interval or even a ratio scale. They may be prepared to assume, for example, that the difference in ability indicated by scores of 20 and 30 is equivalent to the ability difference indicated by scores of 80 and 90 on some well-constructed test, that is, that measurement is on an interval scale. They may be willing to *assume* for instance that when participants in an experiment are instructed to give a number denoting how bright a flash of light seems to them, the numbers they give indicate the strength of their subjective feeling of brightness on a ratio scale, so that someone who responds '20' has experienced a brightness that seems twice as bright as one given the response '10'. Sometimes there is evidence to support such assumptions but it is rarely as convincing as that available for physical measurements.

> **To summarize:**
> ❑ ratio scales tell us more than interval scales;
> ❑ with a ratio scale, equal differences in numbers represent equal differences in the things measured, *and*
> ❑ equal ratios of numbers represent equal ratios in the things measured, so we *can* say that one measured item is twice or three times as great as another;
> ❑ with a ratio scale, a score of zero means that none of the measured property is present.

Absolute scales

The final type is the *absolute* scale. Even though length is measured on a ratio scale so a rod that is twice as long as another gets a score (or measurement) that is twice as great, whatever units are marked on the ruler, the actual *numbers* are different depending on whether the ruler is marked in inches or centimetres, say. But an absolute scale is a ratio scale in which there is no freedom to change even the units of measurement. For all practical purposes that occurs only when we *count* things rather than measure them. It is useful to understand the term, but for most purposes the difference between ratio and absolute scales is not important.

> **To summarize:**
> ❑ absolute scales are ratio scales with the extra property that there is only one possible unit of measurement.

What level of measurement have we achieved?

The purpose of measurement is to represent things by numbers that we can manipulate, tabulate and so on, but the things that interest psychologists are often attributes or abilities that can't be observed directly, such as happiness or general intelligence. We don't *observe* actual happiness or intelligence – only its effects, such as the person smiling or solving problems. When we obtain numbers by measuring something we must always distinguish between the numbers and the things we really want to know about. Numbers are useful only when they allow us to make valid inferences and predictions. The main problem in data analysis is often in deciding in what way, and to what extent, the numbers relate to the questions that really interest us.

The level of measurement that is achieved depends on which relationships between numbers (the order of their sizes for an ordinal scale; the differences between one number and another for an interval scale; the ratios between one number and another for a ratio scale) correspond to properties of the thing measured.

And always remember that the 'thing measured' is the *psychological* or *behavioural* attribute that is being studied. We can measure time on a ratio scale. But it is no good measuring the times people take to solve a problem on a ratio scale unless it is the times themselves that are of interest. If what you really want to know is how intelligent the people are, you probably can *not* assume that the time taken is related to intelligence by better than an ordinal scale (more intelligent people solve the problem faster), so the level of measurement of *intelligence* is only ordinal too.

As another example, whenever we count things, we measure *something* on an absolute scale but it is not always true that what we count is what we want to know about. People often cough more when they're nervous, so if we count how many times a person coughs, it *may* give some indication of how anxious that person is, but it might just indicate an infection or a tickle in the throat. Even if we can be sure that anxiety is the only cause of the coughing, we must be very doubtful about the relationship between the degree of anxiety and the *number of coughs*. We can measure the number of coughs on an absolute scale, but the number of coughs certainly doesn't measure *anxiety* on an absolute scale. At the very best, it may measure it on an ordinal scale where more coughs indicate greater anxiety.

In most psychological measurement we can be pretty sure that our numbers relate to the variable we are interested in by at least an ordinal scale – larger numbers mean that there is more of the thing being measured. It is relatively rare to be confident that measurement is on an interval or ratio scale.

Showing that a psychological quantity is measured on an interval or ratio scale is much more difficult than for most physical scales, such as length or weight. For these, we can take a standard unit, for example a 100 gram weight which we can add to other objects being weighed to show, say, that the difference between 650 and 750 grams is the same as that between 2300 and 2400 grams. We can rarely do anything like that for psychological attributes or behaviour.

Can you think of a way to compare the happiness of different people with a fair degree of confidence? I do not know one, and because of that I do not know any way to measure happiness on a ratio scale, or even on an interval scale. That situation is very common in psychology: measurements are very often made on no better than an ordinal scale, and it is *absolutely essential* to remember that when interpreting results.

The normal curve

In spite of that, we can often argue that measurements are approximately on an interval scale because the scores we obtain turn out to have a particular distribution predicted by mathematical theory. Most psychological variables don't have a single cause but many separate causes. For example, musical ability is probably influenced by several inherited genes and by many different experiences at home and elsewhere. Mathematicians have proved that when a score results from the addition of many, independent, components, a graph of the resulting distribution of frequencies approaches a particular shape called the normal curve. (More information about the normal curve is given in Unit 2 *Describing and Interpreting Data*.) For example, the heights and the weights of the adult population are distributed in a pattern quite similar to the normal curve, because an individual's height or weight is determined by many, independent causes.

We don't need to use that information in order to prove that height and weight are measured on ratio scales because we have better ways of doing it, but it can be a valuable argument when considering a psychological variable. For instance, we might use a particular test to measure the intelligence of a huge and random selection of people. If we then find that the distribution of test scores is close to a normal curve we can take that as evidence that we have measured intelligence on an interval scale, at least approximately. If equal differences in intelligence had been represented by unequal differences in the numbers, the resulting distribution would not have produced a normal curve; the graph would have been distorted.

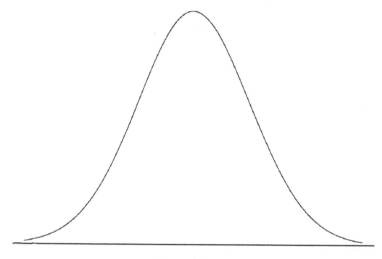

Normal Curve

An example: Albert claimed that Frothibars are ten times as good as Blokkos. **Q:** For the statement to be really meaningful, what level of measurement of 'goodness' would he need to have achieved? Is he likely to have achieved it?

A: Statements about the numerical ratio between two items are meaningful only if they have been measured on a ratio (or absolute) scale. If measurement is only ordinal or interval, no sensible statements can be made about how many times one item exceeds another.

It is possible that the statement may be correct, *for Albert*, and at *that particular time*, because he is speaking about his own feelings and values and he knows about them in a way that we can not, but we have no way to be sure about that. Most likely, he is exaggerating to emphasize his strong preference for Frothibars, and Victoria's offer to swop a Frothibar for five Blokkos is just a way of calling his bluff. She does not expect the offer to be accepted, though if Albert's claim is true he should certainly accept it because he will receive something twice as good (a Frothibar) as the five Blokkos he hands over. Victoria would be pleased with the deal too. (Her preferences are different, and differences in the way that individuals value goods constitute the basis for all trade.)

It is likely that a person's liking for chocolate can be established on no better than an *ordinal* scale, because the attractiveness of a *second* Frothibar is probably less than that of the first. You may prefer apple pie to steak pie and yet prefer one of each to two apple pies. Since our feelings about the goodness of items change according to the circumstances, we *can not* assume that two apple pies are exactly twice as good as one.

SAQ
3

What level of measurement is achievable in measuring each of the following attributes of people? Age; weight; mathematical ability; vocabulary size; family size.

The importance of scale type

Each type of scale I have described – nominal, ordinal, interval, ratio and absolute – has all the properties of the preceding types, and some others that make it more desirable, so whenever it is possible to measure on an absolute, ratio or interval scale we should do so. We lose nothing and the numbers we obtain give us better information about the things measured. If we prefer to treat our results as ordinal, we can do so, even if our measurements are at the interval or ratio level of measurement. But not the other way round: we must not interpret ordinal measurements as though they are at the interval or ratio level.

Summary
- ❏ If measurements are on a *nominal* scale, the numbers tell us if items are the same or different. We can't use the numbers to discover if one item exceeds another or to compare items in any way at all.
- ❏ If measurements are on an *ordinal* scale, the numbers tell us if one item exceeds another, but don't tell us by how much items differ. We can not use the numbers to compare differences between items or ratios of items.
- ❏ If measurements are on an *interval* scale, the numbers tell us if one item exceeds another, and by how much. That is, differences between numbers tell us if the differences between items are large or small. However, the numbers don't tell us about the ratios of items (such as one item having twice the magnitude of another).
- ❏ If measurements are on a *ratio* scale, the numbers tell us everything that an interval scale does and also allow us to say by how many times one item exceeds another. That is, ratios of numbers reflect ratios in the measured items.

4 Observation and experiment

KEY AIMS: By the end of Part 4 you should understand:
  ▷   *the difference between experiments and observational studies;*
  ▷   *what distinguishes both of these from surveys;*
  ▷   *the advantages and disadvantages of each of these types of investigation;*
  ▷   *the wide range of methods available in the social and behavioural sciences.*

> Victoria: Let's go and talk to Jane. That'll cheer her up. I'm sure she's feeling rotten – you'll see she's not angry with you.
> Albert: I don't want to talk to her. I'd rather just wait and see what she does next.

Victoria proposes to do something so that Albert can see how Jane reacts. She thinks she *knows* (a prediction based on her model) how Jane will react and expects her proposed action to turn out to be best for everyone, including Jane. Albert also thinks he knows how it will turn out and, because his model is different and makes a different prediction, he doesn't fancy that outcome at all. His preferred line is to do nothing to affect Jane until he has more information to help him decide between his model of the situation and Victoria's.

Either course of action might give them evidence for one model or the other (though possibly neither model is correct and Jane may surprise them both by bursting out laughing, having just pretended to be angry, or she may turn out to be worried rather than angry or unwell). Of the two kinds of action, Victoria's seems more likely to produce clear evidence one way or the other, but either approach could work and Victoria's has some degree of danger because if her model is wrong, Albert will be upset by the result.

Intervening in a situation to change it in order to see which models are supported and which are eliminated by the results is the essential feature of an **experiment.** The approach of letting matters take their own course and merely noting what happens while doing your best to avoid affecting what goes on, is an **observational study**. It is possible to describe the alternatives discussed by Albert and Victoria in that way but it would be unkind and unfair. They are not *studying* Jane but trying to interact with her socially. To carry out research with people requires a degree of detachment in the investigator, who must stand back from the situation rather than fully participating in it, and that is not what they are doing.

Two words of warning

Partly because the person carrying out an investigation needs to be detached from full social interaction with people who are being studied, it is customary to refer to them as **subjects.** The word is completely neutral in a scientific context and means only that they are the subject of study. But it is wise to remember that although the term is neutral to scientists it may not seem neutral to other people so it should be used with care! Instead of recruiting *subjects* to take part in an investigation it is better to ask for 'volunteers' or 'participants', or just 'people'!

It is important that nobody should use the fact that they are undertaking a social or psychological investigation as an excuse for doing or saying things they would object to if they were done or said by someone else. Even if you are maintaining the necessary degree of detachment for the purpose of the investigation you must remember that some things you might wish to do may run the danger of upsetting, or even harming, others so you must carefully consider the *ethics* of any procedure before adopting it. In fact it is not enough that *you* would not object – *no reasonable person* should object – and bear in mind that even reasonable people may be much more touchy or easily hurt than you are about all sorts of things. Professional organizations such as the British Psychological Society have prepared leaflets to provide carefully-considered guidelines on ethical matters that can arise in conducting investigations with humans and with animals. Another Unit in this series deals in more depth with such ethical issues.

Ways to obtain data

We have considered two broad classes of investigation: recording observations of what would have happened whether or not we were there (observational studies) and making something happen to see what the outcome is (experiment). But there are many approaches to gathering information. We can:

1. record our own thoughts, feelings and mental experiences **(introspection)**;
2. collect observations of things that happen anyway **(observational study)**;
3. record the changes that occur as a particular person grows older **(developmental case study**, or, **longitudinal case study)**;
4. record the changes that occur as someone undergoes therapy **(clinical case study)**;
5. record the changing characteristics of a group over a period of time **(cohort study)**;
6. join a group in order to study it **(participant observation)**;
7. talk to individuals face-to-face **(interview)**;
8. ask questions in writing **(questionnaire study)**;
9. treat participants in different ways and see what the outcome is **(experiment)**.

Participant observation

It is not possible to draw up a complete list of methods. Each of the types listed here can take various forms according to the nature of the participants and the purpose of the investigation. Every method has advantages and disadvantages. Some are equally appropriate to the study of people and of animals and some will only work with people. Each of them works better for some purposes than for others.

SOMETHING TO TRY
For each of the methods listed above, decide if it is:
(a) suitable for use with humans;
(b) suitable for use with animals;
(c) closer to observation or to experiment.

STT answers
(a) All the methods can be used with humans.
(b) Methods 1, 6, 7 and 8 are not suitable for use with animals, and 4 is hardly appropriate.
(c) Methods 1, 2, 3, 4, 5 and 6 would all have the aim of not influencing what happens but merely recording what occurs. Whether or not that can be achieved is always a matter to be considered carefully because the mere fact of observing may change the situation. With methods 1 and 6, it is certain that the procedure creates a changed situation and the central question is the importance of the change. The results of the observations may influence the way a child is treated (in case 3) or the therapy given (in case 4). If so, the observations are again influencing what would otherwise have occurred. However, *none* of these ways in which observing may influence events has the nature of *an experiment* unless the resulting changes are made deliberately to test the predictions of a model.

Advantages of observation and experiment compared

Here are some advantages of observational studies over experiments:
1.   If we have not interfered with the normal course of events we know that the things we observed *do happen in real life*, whereas events in an experiment might not.
2.   We can study events that it would be impossible or unethical to cause to happen.

Here are some advantages of experiments over observational studies:
1.   We can usually repeat an experiment.
2.   We can observe things that would occur very rarely without our intervention.
3.   We can be much more confident about *exactly* what happened because we can control many features of the situation.

The fact that experiments can be repeated is a very important advantage. Suppose you have discovered that people can learn a list of words more easily than an equally long list of numbers and you want to convince someone else about your result. You could wait forever without ever *observing* anyone trying to do that. On the other hand, you can repeat it as *an experiment* any time you can assemble some volunteers and, what is more, you can invite the other person to do it too. That makes the evidence from experiments very convincing. If they have doubts about the outcome they need only repeat it themselves.

Furthermore, because we can repeat experiments, they can convince us about cause and effect: if we get effect B every time we administer condition A, and do not get it when A is *not* administered, we can be sure that A causes B. If we only *observe* that B always follows A it is not at all certain that A *causes* B. Children learn to read after they learn to talk; the year's coldest weather comes after many birds have migrated. In neither of these cases do we believe that the first event *causes* the second, even though the second almost invariably follows the first.

Anecdotal evidence

Events that are merely *observed* to occur cannot be repeated at will, and that makes the evidence less persuasive. That is especially so if the observations are made in an unplanned way. There have been countless reports of extra-sensory perception (ESP), such as telepathy (reading someone's thoughts at a distance) or precognition (foretelling the future). But most scientists are sceptical about them because they are reports of unpredicted events that occurred on particular occasions. Such reports constitute **anecdotal evidence**, that is, evidence consisting of reports of events where it was not expected that the event would occur so no arrangements were made to record exactly what happened. Anecdotal evidence is different from the evidence of observational studies because we did not plan to collect it – the event just happened – so we have to *reconstruct from memory* what happened before the interesting event, and we know that memory can't be relied on. In an observ-ational study, we collect the information in a planned way, so the quality of our record of what preceded an event is as good as our information about the event itself. The evidence from a properly-conducted observational study is *not* anecdotal.

Limits of experimentation

Attempts have been made to study ESP by means of experiments but, if the phenomenon is a real one, it seems that it cannot be repeated at will. Those who believe that ESP is real say that conducting an experiment distorts the conditions that are needed for it to occur. And that is indeed the main problem with experiments. Intervening to control the situation may make the situation unnatural so that what goes on in the laboratory does not reflect the real world. If we are interested in whether people are more likely to forget a spouse's birthday or their wedding anniversary, it is no good trying to carry out an experiment. Drawing attention to the matter will hopelessly distort what would happen in daily life. There is plenty of anecdotal evidence, but scientists don't find that at all persuasive. You just have to conduct some form of observational study or a **survey.**

Some things cannot be studied by experiment because we have no way to make them happen. We cannot make people like each other in order to see if friendships between people of similar age last longer than between those of different ages. And even if we could do it, it would not be ethical to interfere in the lives of others in that way for scientific purposes. There are many things we cannot study by experiment, even though it's perfectly possible to cause them, because it would be unethical to do so. For example, it would not be ethical to cause a fire just to see how people react, but it may be possible to *observe* behaviour in fires that occur by accident.

Surveys

Although experiments and observational studies have important differences, they are alike in one way that distinguishes them from surveys: they both obtain data from the things that people or animals *do*. In **surveys**, the data consist of what people *say* about what they do or what they *say* about their opinions, attitudes, ambitions, relationships – indeed, about any topic on which they can be questioned.

Surveys may be conducted by means of questionnaires: that is, lists of questions supplied in a written form, with answers being written down or chosen from a selection of possible answers by the **respondents** (the people who answer). Surveys can also be conducted by means of personal **interviews**, or in other ways, such as **diary studies** where people record their own actions for later analysis.

Advantages and disadvantages of survey methods

Since the data come from what people tell us rather than from what they are observed to do, there is always a danger of being told lies. Even if people do not tell actual lies, it is often likely that we are not told the whole of the truth. People usually want to show themselves in a good light, so questions about antisocial or embarrassing actions may not receive truthful answers. It is also possible that people *try* to tell the whole truth but are unable to remember everything. For reasons like these, it is quite difficult to obtain really good data by survey methods, and doing so requires a great deal of effort and expertise.

On the other hand, there are many topics that can not realistically be studied in any other way. If we are interested in behaviour that occurred in the past – during the childhood of today's pensioners, say – or in things that happen in private, such as the conversation topics of families eating meals together – we are almost obliged to use survey methods. They can also be the most practicable way to obtain a reasonable amount of data about events that happen rarely. We could *observe* for a very long time before we happen to witness a meeting between friends who have been separated for several years, but many people would be able to *remember* such events and answer questions about how they behaved and how they felt. The alternative of causing such meetings to occur (that is, using the method of *experiment*) would be difficult, and probably unethical. And survey methods would be easier, safer, and more ethical than observational methods for gathering data about behaviour in fires.

(a) *List three important differences between an experiment and an observational study.*

(b) *In what way are experiments and observational studies alike and different from surveys?*

Field and laboratory studies

We usually associate experiments with laboratories and observational studies with the world outside, but that is not always the case. In an **observational field study** we may go out into the world to observe animals living in their natural habitat, or we may watch people going about their daily lives. In each case, we would be taking systematic observations to record what happens without our intervention. The word *field* here indicates that the study is done *away from the laboratory*. But it is also possible to conduct a **field experiment**, in which we make a deliberate change in the real world to see how it influences the behaviour of the people or animals we are trying to understand. For example, bees have been caught while gathering nectar and kept in the dark for several hours to see if the direction they fly in when released is affected by the changed position of the sun in the sky.

Conversely, even in the laboratory we may merely *observe* what our subjects do without taking any action that might influence them, in an **observational laboratory study**. Research on the inheritance of psychological attributes such as anxiety and inquisitiveness in rats has made considerable use of the technique of observing and recording in detail the movements the rats made in a miniature arena when left alone there. (It is perhaps a little confusing that this laboratory procedure is called the *open-field test!*) The advantage of performing the observations in the laboratory rather than in the world outside is only partly its convenience. More important is the possibility it gives of ensuring that the circumstances are equivalent on every occasion the observations are made, so that differences can be attributed to the subjects rather than to variables in the environment.

SAQ
5

For each of the topics listed, indicate the appropriateness of experiment, observational study, and survey as methods of scientific investigation.
(a) People's belief in the existence of 'flying saucers'.
(b) The relative effectiveness of two medicines in curing headaches.
(c) People's tendency to pass each other on the right or on the left when walking on pavements.

A POSSIBLE PROJECT

Most behavioural topics can be studied in several, quite different, ways. Design an experiment, an observational study and a survey to investigate the relationship between fatigue and the accuracy of memory. All three designs should involve about the same amount of effort and expense to carry out. For each of the designs, identify its good features and its bad features relative to the other two designs.

Summary
- For any particular topic being investigated, there are many ways to collect data. Which is best depends on all the circumstances and several approaches may be equally suitable.
- Methods can be classified into three broad groups: experiments; observational studies; surveys.
- In experiments, we cause something to happen and record the consequences.
- In observational studies, we do our best to avoid affecting what happens and merely record in a planned way what does happen.
- In surveys, we ask questions and record the answers that are given.
- Evidence from experiments is persuasive because they can be repeated if necessary but because they require intervention, they may not reflect what happens in natural conditions.
- Evidence from observational studies represents what does actually occur in natural circumstances, but the events can not be repeated at will.
- Evidence from surveys consists of what people say rather than what they do, so there is a possibility of being deceived, accidentally or deliberately, by respondents. However, some topics cannot reasonably be investigated in any other way.

Problems in all data collection:
Objectivity, Reactivity, Sampling

KEY AIMS: By the end of Part 5 you should understand:
▷   *the difference between objective and subjective evidence;*
▷   *how objectivity can be increased;*
▷   *how behaviour can be altered by being studied;*
▷   *the desirability of obtaining unbiased samples;*
▷   *some ways of obtaining satisfactory samples.*

Albert: It's true that people look like their pets. Look at Mr. Thorpe's dog.
Victoria: Mr. Thorpe doesn't look like a Collie. He's more of a Red Setter.
Albert: Well, Mrs Thorpe is definitely a Collie.
Victoria: She's an Old English Sheepdog!

It's unlikely that Albert and Victoria can settle the argument. They can't agree whether people do or don't look like their pets because they don't even agree about what the evidence is. Quite literally, they may *see things differently*. They are only joking – drawing parallels between the Thorpes and particular dog breeds the way a cartoonist emphasizes features to make an amusing caricature – but the problem is common in science: can you obtain evidence that is **objective**, that is, information that doesn't depend on personal interpretation and opinion? (**Subjective** evidence depends on personal feelings or on ideas that others may not share, so it isn't persuasive.)

Objectivity

People can draw different inferences from the same evidence if they interpret it according to different models. But they may also disagree about what the evidence is. Part 1 looked at some descriptive words and said that some descriptions (such as *heavier*) would, and some (such as *nicer*) would not, be agreed to by any reasonable person. The difference is in their objectivity. When we collect data it should be objective, if that is at all possible. Consider the following example.

Railway Station Study

You are planning an observational field study in a railway station to see if the new ticket-vending machines are satisfactory. From an unobtrusive spot several yards away you will watch people entering the station and going to ticket-sale windows or to the new machines. You plan to note down behaviour that seems to relate to the effectiveness of the machines.

SOMETHING TO TRY

Some things you have thought of recording are listed below. For each of them, indicate if the observation is objective or subjective before reading on.

		Objective	Subjective
1.	Wanting to buy a ticket.	O	O
2.	Obtaining a ticket from a machine.	O	O
3.	Hurrying.	O	O
4.	Having difficulty finding money.	O	O
5.	Becoming confused.	O	O

STT Answers

Only item 2 is truly objective. Anyone in a position to see the ticket being taken from the machine should agree about it.

Item 1 is an inference because it is just your opinion about the *purpose* that another person has for actions that were actually observed. Even if it is very reasonable, an inference isn't objective.

Item 3 is an absolute, quantitative term, so observers may disagree about what speed of movement should be described as 'hurrying'. The evidence is therefore subjective. You might be able to measure the time from entering the station to reaching the machine. That would be objective but wouldn't really measure 'hurrying' because it depends on various factors apart from speed, such as how well the passenger knows the station and some people move faster than others even when they are not 'hurrying'.

Items 4 and 5 are both interpretations to explain the behaviour that can be observed objectively. Other observers might interpret the same behaviour differently, such as the passenger suddenly realising that something important has been forgotten, so the interpretations are subjective. The same might even be true of Item 2. It would *not* be objective to record a ticket being taken from the machine if you could only watch from behind as someone approached the machine, made some movements, and walked away. That would be an **inference** from what you had actually observed. Interpretations of data should be made after collecting the data, not *while* collecting it.

Before reading further, can you suggest modifications that would improve the design of the study?

Improving objectivity

Whenever there is room for observers to disagree about whether an event has occurred or not, it is better to select other events that convey the same information without disagreements. But sometimes no objective observations can capture the essence of what we want to know. For example, if you are studying social interactions you can probably decide objectively when someone is *speaking* but perhaps not always for *smiling* or *frowning*. Yet smiling and frowning may be an important part of the way people interact and can't just be ignored by a researcher. If so, the best plan is to have several observers recording the events *independently*. In that way, you can discover which they agree on and you can be reasonably confident about these results even though they are not objective.

Reactivity: The effects of being studied

The description of the Railway Station Study said that you planned to watch from an unobtrusive spot several yards away. Perhaps you think that isn't such a good idea and it would be better to stand beside the machines so you can see what happens really clearly? If you do that, it is pretty well certain that you will affect the behaviour of passengers. Perhaps some who do not feel confident about using the machines decide not to use them today because you are watching. Perhaps others who might have used them will go to the ticket windows because they think you are part of a queue. Perhaps some passengers who would have had difficulty with the machines will ask you for help. These effects may be important for the outcome of your study and they are changes *caused by the mere fact that you are watching*. Because you have changed the situation for the participants and they react to that change, the term used is **reactivity.**

Some examples of reactivity

- ❑ White and black interviewers obtain different answers to questions concerning race.
- ❑ People who know that they are being observed are less likely to cheat in a test than those who do not.
- ❑ Investigators who expect a certain outcome in an experiment are more likely to obtain it than those who expect a different outcome.
- ❑ Participants who believe that they have taken a drug that affects the way they feel react differently from those who believe that they have had a sugar pill, even if both groups have sugar pills.

Can you think of other examples of reactivity in behavioural research?

Combating reactivity

It isn't possible to obtain results without carrying out some form of observation – and that always carries the danger of changing the situation in ways that cause reactivity. One possibility is to minimize the situational change caused by measurement. (In the Railway Station Study this is achieved by observing from a discreet distance.) In an experiment, participants almost always know that they are being studied and that can cause reactivity that we can not eliminate.

Placebos and placebo groups

If it's impossible to disguise the *fact* of being observed, another method is to generate the same circumstances for two or more groups, with a difference in treatment of which the participants do not know the details. For example, to evaluate a drug that relieves depression we might give every participant a pill that looks the same, though half have the drug while half contain something that has no effect. The 'dummy' pill is called a **placebo.** The mere fact of being given any medication is known to change the way that patients feel. That is called the **placebo effect** and it is universal practice in medical trials to include a **placebo group** who are given a 'dummy' medication. For the test drug to be shown to be effective, the group that get it must show a bigger improvement than the group given the placebo.

"I hear one of them is a placebo"

If the aim is to *compare* two drugs, a placebo isn't needed. Each group has one of the drugs and we can focus on the difference between their results. If the placebo effect occurs, as it probably will, it can be assumed to affect both groups equally so the difference reflects the different effects of the drugs.

Control groups

The term 'placebo' is mainly used in connection with medical trials. It can be used in a more general sense but in non-medical experiments it is more usual to speak of a **control group** than a 'placebo group'. The terms are very similar in meaning. A control group are not given the particular experimental condition that is being investigated and their scores are used as a baseline with which to compare the scores of the group given the experimental condition. Everything except the actual experimental treatment should apply equally to both the experimental group and the control group. For example, they should be sampled in the same way, should have the same information, the same reward (if any), and should be tested at equivalent times. In that way we hope to ensure that any difference between the experimental group and the control group can be attributed to the one respect in which their treatment differed: the experimental condition.

Blind trials and...

For ethical reasons we should always tell participants what conditions occur in a study they volunteer for and, wherever possible, we should also tell them in advance why the study is being done. Doing so brings a danger of reactivity but it need not be a problem. We can tell participants what all the conditions *are,* but need not say which condition they will actually have. The participants are then said to be **blind** to the experimental conditions. For example, if they do not know which drug (or placebo) they receive their reactions can not be affected by the knowledge.

"Dr. Burns, are you sure this is what the statisticians call a "double blind experiment"?

..double-blind trials

It's even possible that if the *experimenter* knows which group each participant is in, the way the participant is spoken to or treated may be subtly different. For that reason, it is often advisable to use a **double-blind** procedure where the experimenter too doesn't know which group the participant belongs to. That can be achieved in the drug study by having a helper put all the pills into containers with labels whose codes are unknown to the person interacting with the participants. Ideally, the coding would not be revealed until after all the data had been collected and the results analysed.

Can you think of other situations where it would be wise to employ a blind or double-blind technique?

Sampling

Suppose that for your Railway Station Study you are going to minimize reactivity by being unobtrusive and will record a list of objective events to be interpreted later to discover how people use the ticket machines. The next question is, when do you collect observations? If you go along to the station only at convenient times, the passengers you observe may not be typical. Perhaps morning travellers are different from those at midday. Perhaps those at weekends are different from those on weekdays. The times that suit you best may be times when the travelling public are very different from average.

Biased sampling

The difficulty is that you want to know about a very much larger group of passengers than you can possibly observe. Those you observe will be only a **sample** drawn from the **population** of passengers. Note that the term *population* needn't refer to all the people in the country but, as in this example, is usually a subgroup. Let's say that in the present study it is *railway passengers using a particular station* you want to learn about. Your sample may be different from that population in various ways. Young travellers may have no difficulty with the machines while older travellers find them difficult to use. Old and young may be present in your sample in proportions different from those in the population, and if so your conclusions will show **bias** as a result of your **biased sampling**. (Describing a sample as biased does not suggest that the investigator is dishonest or unfair, only that the characteristics of the sample don't accurately reflect those of the population.) It is always undesirable for a sample to be biased unless the bias is so well understood that it can be allowed for when interpreting the results.

Opportunity samples

Methods for obtaining an unbiased sample give every member of the target population a chance of being in the sample. If you had wanted to know about *all railway passengers* rather than those using a particular station, the study could only give a biased sample however well you sample from that one station. Thus whether or not a sample is biased depends on the population we want to know about. If we were interested in all railway passengers, our local station would provide an **opportunity sample** of passengers: that is, a sample who happen to be available for study. Other examples of opportunity samples are: our friends, a club we belong to, a school we attend, and so on. An opportunity sample is always likely to be biased relative to any wider population we may be interested in.

Self-selected samples

Suppose your Railway Station Study never finds anyone having difficulty with the machines. Would that indicate that the machines are entirely satisfactory? Unfortunately, no. Passengers can choose to go to ticket windows instead and those who are wary of the machines may do so. That means that those using the machines are a **self-selected sample** and are likely to consist of people who *prefer* the machines to the ticket windows. Probably those who choose to use the machines do so because they do not expect to have any difficulty with them – perhaps having used them successfully in the past. Those who go to the ticket windows may be different, and if so those using the machines are a biased sample of the relevant population. It's almost always the case that self-selected samples (for example, volunteers) are biased in *some* ways, but the bias isn't necessarily one that has any relevance to the topic being studied. In this case however, the bias is bound to be related to the topic being investigated and the results must be interpreted accordingly.

What can be done if a sample is biased?

If we cannot eliminate bias we can sometimes estimate its effect and draw conclusions about the population that take account of it. For example, if we find that our sample has a higher proportion of young people than the target population we want to know about, we can analyse separately the results from different age groups and use the answers to estimate the population's characteristics by using the results in proportion to the numbers of each age group in the target population. How well that works depends on how much we know about the various ways the sample differs from the population. Age might not be the only form of discrepancy.

For many sources of bias, such as opportunity samples and self-selected samples, such adjustment isn't possible because we don't know exactly what characteristics influenced membership of the sample. In that case we must *redefine the population*. That means we do not draw conclusions about all passengers, say, but only about the population of passengers *who choose the ticket machines*. In that case, we have not answered the original question but a new one.

Aiming to avoid bias

There's no way to avoid all possibility of *accidental* bias in any sampling scheme, but the likelihood of important bias can be greatly reduced. One approach is to take **representative samples** by following a systematic scheme that selects a certain number of each type of participant so as to reflect their frequency in the population. Another approach is to take **random samples** and these too aim to reflect the composition of the population. It may seem strange that what look like opposite approaches (planning what kind of subject to recruit as opposed to choosing them at random) can have the same aim, but that is the case, though they tend to be applied in different situations. And they both differ in an important way from the first sampling scheme that was mentioned – sampling at times that suit the investigator. That scheme had the risk that the composition of the sample would be affected *systematically* by something other than the relative frequency of different types of passenger, while representative and random sampling do not.

Quota samples

One type of representative sample, the **quota sample**, is sometimes used in surveys in the street. The organizer gives each interviewer a list of types of people – for example, men under 30, men over 30, women under 30, women over 30, but usually a much longer list than that, to be interviewed and says how many (what *quota*) of each type should be questioned. In order to fulfil these quotas the interviewer may have to miss out many who pass by if they are of a type whose quota has already been completed, while waiting for someone with just the right characteristics to come along.

True random samples from the general population are quite difficult, and therefore expensive, to obtain. One method is to select names from the *Electoral Register*, making sure that names are selected from all parts of the *Register* so as not to concentrate on people from one district. After the names have been obtained, the researcher has to visit the homes of the people selected and obtain their cooperation. Several visits may be needed before the particular person is found at home. Inevitably, some people will refuse to take part or may have moved away or even died, so the sample can never be entirely unbiased. The *Electoral Register* does not contain names of everyone, and in particular does not list people much below voting age. However, most other lists of possible participants, such as school registers or club membership lists, are even more biased.

SAQ
6

An investigation of people's eating habits was conducted by interviewing shoppers leaving a supermarket and asking the following question. 'Have you bought any food today that is inclined to be fattening?' Identify any problems of objectivity, reactivity and sampling in the study and suggest ways of minimizing these problems.

Summary
- ❑ Scientific evidence should always be as objective as possible.
- ❑ When collecting observational data, we should record what is observed to happen not inferences we make from these observations.
- ❑ We should try to minimize reactivity whenever possible (for example, by making observations inconspicuously).
- ❑ In an experiment, we can often minimize reactivity by using a blind or double-blind procedure.
- ❑ In an experiment, reactivity can never be completely avoided but we can often allow for its effects by using a placebo group (or control group).
- ❑ Samples chosen for investigation should be unbiased (that is, not systematically different from the population we want to know about).

Disentangling possible causes

KEY AIMS: By the end of Part 6 you should understand:
▷   *the different types of variable in an investigation;*
▷   *the need to prevent some kinds of variation;*
▷   *the importance of preventing variables from always changing in step;*
▷   *the need to evaluate the likelihood of obtaining similar results by chance alone.*

Albert: Your photographs are great! These are much better than the first set you showed me. Did you get a new camera?
Victoria: No, it's the same camera, but I tried a new film, and anyway I've learned more. The others are the first I ever took.
Albert: Did the film make a big difference or is it mainly that you've improved?
Victoria: I think it's mainly me. And I took them in Crete where the weather's always good and there are lots of things to photograph.

They are trying to identify what made Victoria's second set of pictures so much better and have considered several possibilities: the camera, the film, her increased skill, the location and the weather. No doubt there are other factors too.

They can rule out the camera as an explanation because that was the same for both sets of pictures, but they can't rule out any of the others, which had all changed. There is yet another possibility they have not considered, but which must always be taken into account in a question of this kind: was it luck? In both sets there are probably some good pictures and some not so good. Saying the second set is better means that pictures in that set are *mostly* better – an aggregate conclusion which may not be true of each picture. It's possible that because she takes some good pictures and some poor ones, she might still take a set with mainly poor ones even now that she has learned a bit more and even if she went back to Crete and used the same type of film.

Confounding variables

Has Victoria improved? Victoria believes that her own improvement was the most important factor, but can she prove that? Well, not on the evidence we have here. There are several possible explanations because several things changed between the first and the second set of photographs. When that happens, when there are several uncontrolled variables, their effects are said to be **confounded** and there is no way to identify what contribution each one makes to the results. If we wish to investigate the question scientifically it's now too late to do so with Victoria, but we could set up a study with someone else new to photography and compare the first pictures with a set taken later. If we are interested in how much improvement is shown by the photographer, it will help if we can stop other things from varying. The usual way to express that is to say that *other variables are held constant*. That is, things that *might* vary (variables) are not allowed to.

Independent, dependent and nuisance variables

Something that might affect the results if it is allowed to vary, but which we do not at present wish to investigate, is called a **nuisance variable**. We can deal

33

with nuisance variables in two ways: we can *hold them constant* or, alternatively, we can *measure their effects* and then allow for them when we interpret other variables. If we hold them constant, we prevent them from having different effects on different sets of data, which simplifies the subsequent analysis. That is the preferable approach unless we are quite sure we know how to make an appropriate allowance for their effects if we allow them to vary.

In an experiment, the **independent variable** is manipulated by the experimenter and the **dependent variable** is the result that is measured. We usually think of the independent variable causing, or at any rate *influencing*, the dependent variable. In relation to the question we are considering here, the dependent variable is the quality of the photographs (indicating the amount by which Victoria has improved) and the independent variable is the time that elapsed between taking the two sets of pictures. All the other variables (the film, the camera, the place, and so on) are nuisance variables, some of which were, and some of which weren't, held constant. A variable that is held constant is sometimes said to be **controlled.**

Controlling nuisance variables

But whether a variable is an independent, a dependent or a nuisance variable *depends on the question we are trying to answer*. If we want to discover if photographs taken in Crete are better than those taken at home, *location* is the independent variable and Victoria's improvement (if any) is one of the *nuisance* variables – if she improved between the first and the later set, it is impossible to say how much of the difference in quality is attributable to the location.

If the question to be answered from the evidence given by the two sets of photographs taken by Victoria is whether photographs taken in good weather are better or worse than those taken in bad weather:

- *which of the variables mentioned – the quality of the photographs, the time between taking the two sets of pictures, the film, the camera, the place, the weather, the skill of the photographer – is the independent variable?*
- *which is the dependent variable?*
- *which are nuisance variables?*

SOMETHING TO TRY
(a)   *Jot down a list of variables that might affect the quality of a particular person's photographs.*
(b)   *For each of these variables, try to invent a way to keep it constant between the first set and a later one.*
(c)   *What other problems do you expect to have in designing the investigation?*

Variables to consider: Subject variables and situational variables

Some nuisance variables that we might want to hold constant are: the camera, the film, the processing firm, the size of print, the place, the subject matter, the time of year, the weather, the amount of effort made by the photographer.

It's easy to ensure that the camera, film, processor and size of print are the same both times. For the time of year we could have the second set taken either very soon after the first or exactly a year later. The second possibility is more trouble but gives more time for improvement to occur. For place, subject matter and weather, we could ask the photographer to take pictures of the same things and only on sunny days or only on cloudy days. We could make both time of year and weather unimportant variables if we ask the photographer to take pictures only indoors in artificial light. It is not at all easy to ensure that the photographer tries equally hard on each occasion. We can't even predict with any confidence on which occasion more effort will be made. Sometimes, variables just cannot be held constant. If we think they are important we can repeat the study several times. In the present case, we would use different people each time and hope that differences in effort would balance out across the group, some making more effort on the first occasion and others on the second.

Measurement variables

Which pictures are best? It's not at all certain that people will agree about which photographs *are* best. In books and magazines you may see the work of expert photographers whose pictures someone must admire but which you don't like at all. You may think them ugly, or even badly taken – blurred or underexposed! So the first problem to solve is how to measure the quality of the photographs. There is nothing objective we can measure that tells us how good a picture is. The usual solution is to have *several independent judges*. A group of people assembled to assess something that can't be measured in any other way is often referred to as a **panel** of assessors or judges. The average of the ratings they give can not be taken to be a picture's true merit, if there is such a thing, but at least it's a measure that approximately reflects what most people think of it. The point about them being *independent* is that the judgements of one should not influence the judgements of another. Unless that happens, we lose much of the benefit of having several judges. In the extreme case, if one judge states an opinion and all the others just agree with it, you learn no more than if you had used the first judge alone. To ensure independence, the panel should make their judgements quite separately and not know what other judges think about any of the pictures.

There is another problem to solve in measuring the quality of the pictures. Suppose the first set of pictures are rated by the panel, then a year later the photographer takes another set which are then rated by the same panel. Can we be sure that any difference in the ratings is because the photographer has changed? Of course not – it may be the panel whose tastes have changed. The problem is not much better if the two occasions are closer in time.

SOMETHING TO TRY
Before reading further, write down a procedure for judging the two sets of photographs that would allow an investigator to overcome the problem that the panel's tastes may change.

Using a panel to judge photographs taken at different times. The best way to deal with the possibility that the panel's tastes may change is to have both sets rated not only by the same panel but at the same time. The photographs should be mixed together and judged as one set. Only afterwards should the scores for the two sets be separated. That has two advantages: not only are the sets judged more or less simultaneously but it's possible to judge them *blind*: the judges needn't know to which set a picture belongs. It's possible that a judge who knew that a certain picture was one of the first the photographer had taken might give it a different rating as a result. We might even use a double-blind technique and not inform the person who gives the judge the pictures.

Order effects. It would also be a good idea to present the pictures to each judge in a different order. In that way, we reduce even further the possibility that pictures in one set have their average ratings affected by the sequence in which they are judged, since it is different for each judge. **Order effects** are a very common type of nuisance variable when more than one score comes from each individual. The score obtained on the second occasion may be either higher or lower just as a result of being obtained second. For example, Victoria's second set of photographs may actually *be* better, and thus earn higher scores, because of what she learned by taking the first set rather than because of some other factor we are investigating – or judges may *tend to award lower scores* to the second set of photographs because their standards have been influenced as a result of judging the first set.

To counteract order effects we can either **randomize** the order of presentation or **counterbalance** it. Randomizing involves presenting the conditions in an order selected by chance for each participant, for example, by tossing a coin. Counterbalancing involves ensuring that each possible order occurs equally often, preferably by drawing up a balanced testing plan in advance. Both methods are satisfactory, but one may be more convenient than the other in any particular case.

Randomizing the order of presentation is analogous to drawing a random sample of participants: both procedures allow *chance* to determine what occurs. Counterbalancing the order of presentation is analogous to taking a representative sample: both *follow a plan* to ensure that each type of participant, or each order of presentation, occurs a predetermined number of times.

Chance as a possible explanation

One of the possibilities overlooked by Albert and Victoria was that the difference between the two sets might have been pure chance. We have been discussing how to carry out a study to test the model that a photographer's skill changes over time. If we collect results to see if the predictions of a model are fulfilled, there is no problem if the model makes an exact prediction and the study provides an exact answer. But in earlier sections we have had to accept that in psychology and other behavioural sciences, neither need be true. We just don't have any models that say precisely what an individual will do. Psychological models say things like: *Group A is more likely to get high scores than Group B*. If Group B obtains a higher average than Group A, that does not actually contradict the model. The model just says that the result is *unlikely*. Still, a result that the model says is unlikely tends to make us doubt the model.

Even if we are certain about our data, we cannot say for certain that the observed results disagree with a model whose predictions are not exact. It might seem that the idea of testing models to see if they predict events will not work because chance outcomes can give an adequate explanation for anything we observe. Fortunately, that is not so. Any model of human or animal behaviour must include some uncertainty, because we can never know enough about living things to be entirely sure what they will do. But it is possible to describe that uncertainty in quite precise ways.

Taking good photographs by chance

All photographers take some good pictures and some bad ones. Experts take very few bad ones and novices take few good ones, but even novices can take the occasional picture that everyone admires. We can express that by saying that the **probability** of taking good pictures is greater for experts than for novices and (provided that we have agreed how to decide whether or not a picture is good) we can say what the probability of taking a good picture is for any individual photographer. A probability is a number between 0, (indicating that he or she never takes any good photographs) and 1, (indicating that he or she never takes any bad ones). A probability of 0.2 means that there are, on average, two good ones in every ten. Something we might want to do is estimate the probability of one of Victoria's photographs being described as 'good'. Because there is an element of chance in her success rate, we will not be sure about the exact value of the estimate we make, but we will become more sure as the amount of data increases. Something else we might want to know is if her photography has improved and her pictures now have a greater probability of being considered 'good' than when she began.

Eliminating chance as an explanation for a difference

Suppose that in her first film Victoria had 5 good pictures out of 24 and in her later one she had 13 good ones, a difference of 8. We can calculate the probability of getting a difference of 8 *or more* if, in fact, the probability of taking good pictures was *the same* for each film. The idea that there is *no difference* between two conditions or two groups of subjects is also a model, called the **null model.** More frequently it is referred to as the **null hypothesis.**

OLD METHODS OF
MARKING EXAMS
WERE SOMEWHAT
CRUDE ....

BUT WITH THE
DEVELOPMENT OF
MODERN
SCIENTIFIC
TECHNIQUES....

We don't usually need to do the hard part of the calculations ourselves because mathematicians have worked out all the probabilities already, so all we need to do is look up the answers in **statistical tables** that they have prepared. Such tables come in many forms and can be used in various ways. There are statistical tables in Unit 3, *Drawing Inferences from Statistical Data*, which also describes how to calculate a **statistic** called chi-squared (usually written χ^2 and pronounced 'Kye') that is used to obtain the probability needed for this example, and how to interpret the result it gives.

By calculating chi-squared and referring to a suitable statistical table, we can find the probability of getting results of the kind we did get if the null hypothesis is true, that is, if the probability of good pictures is equal for each film. If we find that such results are very unlikely, we reject the null model and conclude that the probability of good pictures has changed. In that way, we have eliminated chance (or luck) as an explanation for Victoria's greater success with the later film. It's not that the model has been found to be unlikely but that *if the model is true we have obtained results that are very unlikely* (and that is not the same thing at all).

If we decide that the null hypothesis cannot explain a difference we have observed unless we accept that our study has produced some extremely unlikely results – 'why should something so unlikely happen to *me*?' – we say that we have observed a **significant** (or **statistically significant**) difference and can reject the null hypothesis. The important point is that even if a model contains random components that make it possible for almost any outcome to occur, some of these outcomes are so improbable *according to the model itself* that, if they happen, the model practically has to be rejected.

If we find that the difference is *not* very unlikely, according to the null hypothesis, we have to conclude that the null model cannot be rejected. We haven't shown that it's *true*, because there may be many other models that also agree quite well with the results, but because we can't reject the null model, we cannot eliminate chance as a reasonable explanation. And if chance can't be eliminated as the source of our results, it's impossible to make a convincing argument in favour of a different explanation so there's not much point in any further interpretation of the data.

One thing we might do, though, is *collect more data*, because a possible reason for results being non-significant is having not enough data to reach a firm conclusion.

Designing good studies

In Part 6 we have been considering ways of separating out the many explanations for a result that may at first seem to be possible. We do so because it is only by eliminating other explanations that we are left with a single, clear conclusion. If many possible explanations are confounded it is not possible to conclude that any particular one of them is responsible for what has been observed. Some alternative explanations can be eliminated by designing the study to remove confounding variables or by holding nuisance variables constant. Almost always, chance is a possibility that cannot be removed entirely even by good design because it is a necessary part of the models we are evaluating. However, statistical analysis gives us a way of eliminating chance as a *plausible* explanation even if it can never eliminate it as a *possible* one.

But it is only if we can imagine all possible explanations before we carry out the study that we can design studies where they are not confounded. That is a great deal to ask. It's a skill for which some people have a natural talent but at which we can all become better by practice. While reading about studies that other people have done, we should think about why they did things in the particular way they describe: what possible confounding effects were they trying to avoid? We may even spot possible confounding variables that the authors have missed. Certainly when we plan studies ourselves, we must spend quite a long time thinking about ways that the results might turn out, about how we would want to interpret such results and about the existence of confounding variables that may make it impossible for us to draw clear conclusions.

Although it is a very important ingredient, the ability to design good studies is not the only thing necessary for good science. We must also pick good problems to investigate and be able to select or invent models creatively to account for what is observed and give us the kind of understanding that makes it possible to predict other phenomena before we have actually observed them.

Summary
- If two or more variables change together, they are said to be *confounded* and it is impossible to say which of them is responsible for any results that are observed.
- *Independent* variables are those that are manipulated in an experiment.
- *Dependent* variables are those that are observed as the outcome of an experiment.
- *Nuisance* variables are those we do not at present want to study but which are capable of affecting the results.
- *Controlled* variables are those we prevent from varying in case they affect the results.
- If the results depend on personal opinion, we can make them more nearly objective by using averages from a *panel* of judges. Where possible, it is even better to use only the results that all the panel agree about.
- Any outcome can occur by chance alone, though some outcomes are very unlikely. We need to test the *statistical significance* of a result to decide if it could easily be caused by chance or if, instead, we need some other explanation.
- If chance could reasonably explain the results, we say that the result is *not significant* and we need not look for any other explanation.

GLOSSARY

Absolute quantitative term: an expression such as 'big' or 'fast' which describes the size or strength of something without comparing it to anything else.

Absolute scale: a ratio scale in which the unit of measurement is fixed. Numbers on an absolute scale are practically always obtained by counting something.

Aggregate conclusion: an answer which is true on average but is not necessarily true of every individual. See also 'Existential conclusion' and 'General conclusion'.

Anecdotal evidence: evidence obtained informally from isolated incidents rather than as part of a systematic investigation.

Assume: take to be true without evidence, or with very inadequate evidence.

Bias: any tendency for results to differ from the true value in some consistent way. Bias should be distinguished from random error, which does not occur in any particular direction.

Biased sample: a sample selected in a way that makes some individuals in the population more likely than others to be included in the sample.

Blind study: one in which the participants do not know the details of the materials they are responding to or the nature of the difference between one experimental condition and another. See also, 'double-blind study'.

Case study: an investigation based on the detailed study of a single individual.

Clinical case study: a case study conducted in connection with therapy.

Cohort study: an investigation based on detailed study, usually over an extended period of time, of a group (or cohort) of individuals.

Confounding: a defect in the design of a study whereby two or more variables change together, with the result that we cannot tell which of them is responsible for any effects that are observed.

Control group: a group of participants in an experiment who are treated in the same way as the experimental group except in one particular respect which is the topic of the experiment. To interpret the outcome of the experiment, we compare the results of the experimental group with those of the control group.

Controlled variable: something that might have varied in a study but has been prevented from varying in order to eliminate any effect it might have had on the results.

Counterbalance: When a nuisance variable (such as participants' improvement with practice) can not be eliminated from a study it is sometimes possible to counterbalance it. That is, we make its effects operate equally on all the other conditions, for example, by administering the various tasks in different orders.

Deduce: arrive at a conclusion by calculation or the use of logic.

Dependent variable: a variable in a study whose value is influenced by the state of some other variable, called the 'independent variable'. Dependent variables are those that are measured to provide the results in an experiment.

Developmental case study: a case study recording the increasing capabilities of a child or young animal as it matures.

Diary study: a technique of investigation in which participants record their own activities for subsequent analysis and interpretation.

Double-blind study: one in which neither the participants nor the person who administers the study knows the details of the materials or the conditions being presented in each particular case. See also, 'blind study'.

Existential conclusion: an answer which shows that something exists or can occur, even if it is observed only rarely. See also 'Aggregate conclusion' and 'General conclusion'.

Experiment: a method of investigation in which one or several 'independent variables' are manipulated in order to discover their effect on one or more 'dependent variables'.

Field experiment: an experiment conducted in the normal environment of the participants.

Field study: an investigation, usually involving observation rather than experiment, conducted in the normal environment of the participants.

Frequency: in data analysis, means the number of times that a particular type of result occurs.

General conclusion: an answer which is true of every individual. See also 'Aggregate conclusion' and 'Existential conclusion.

Hypothesis: an explanation that is considered to be possible but is not known to be correct.

Independent variable: a variable which influences one or more 'dependent variables'. Independent variables are those that are manipulated by someone conducting an experiment.

Inference: a conclusion reached by a process of calculation or logical deduction.

Interval scale: a scale of measurement in which we know that equal differences between numbers indicate equal differences in the attribute that is measured, but we do not know what numerical value corresponds to complete absence of the attribute.

Interview: a method of collecting data by face-to-face or telephone questioning of one person by another.

Introspection: a method of collecting data where we record and comment on our own feelings and internal experiences.

Investigation: a broad term referring to any method of collecting data, such as experiments, surveys, interviews and so on (equivalent to 'study').

Longitudinal case study: a case study recording the changes that occur in the characteristics of someone with the passage of time.

Measurement model: the relationship that we believe or assume to exist between an attribute that we wish to measure and the numbers describing the attribute.

Measurement: the process of representing attributes of people, of events or of things by numbers in a systematic way.

Model: a representation of an organism, a relationship, an event or a process in a way that is simpler than the original. Models can be concrete (composed of actual substances) such as 'model boats' or abstract (consisting only of theoretical elements, numbers and relationships, for example) such as the 'null model'.

Nominal scale: the use of numbers purely as names for the category that an object or event belongs to. The sizes of the numbers tell us nothing about the properties of the object or event.

Normal curve: a mathematical curve which is important in statistics because it has been proved to be the shape of distribution expected when a large number of independent causes add together to produce an outcome. As a result, many attributes of humans and animals, such as height and weight, have frequency distributions that approximately follow a normal curve.

Nuisance variable: a variable we do not want to know about but which is capable of influencing the variables we do want to know about. In designing studies, we either aim to prevent nuisance variables from influencing the results or we design the study in such a way that the effects of nuisance variables can be measured and allowed for.

Null hypothesis: a statistical model which accounts for any observed results by attributing them to chance alone. The probability of obtaining such results if the null hypothesis is correct is called the 'significance' of the results. If the probability is small (by convention, anything less than 0.05) the result is said to be 'significant' and the null hypothesis is rejected in favour of some other model which attributes at least part of the effect to something other than chance. See 'significance test' and 'statistical significance'.

Null model: another term for the null hypothesis.

Numerical model: a model using numbers and the relations among them. See also 'measurement model' which is the most common type of numerical model.

Objective: describes something whose truth or falsity can be demonstrated convincingly to anyone. It is contrasted with 'subjective'.

Observational study: an investigation where data is collected by observing events as they occur and, so far as possible, without influencing them. An observational field study is conducted in the natural environment of the subjects while an observational laboratory study is conducted under controlled conditions.

Opportunity sample: a sample consisting of a group that already exists, such as a social club or a school class.

Order effect: an influence on results brought about by the order in which procedures are administered or measurements are taken.

Ordinal scale: a measurement scale in which larger numbers indicate more of the measured attribute, but neither the size of the difference between two numbers nor the ratio of two numbers tells us anything useful about the attributes.

Panel: a group of people organized to judge something in a situation where individuals might give different answers. Even when the judgement of an individual would be subjective, the average judgment of the panel, and especially any judgments they all agree about, is closer to being objective.

Participant: a person whose actions or attributes form part of the results. The term 'subject' is more usual in the case of animals.

Participant observation: a method of data collection where the investigator takes part in the activities of a group while recording events that occur.

Placebo: a dummy therapy or medicine which, as far as the participants in the study are concerned, is indistinguish-able from a real therapy or medicine.

Placebo effect: any effect produced by a participant's knowledge or belief about the nature of an investigation. The most typical placebo effect is an improvement produced by giving a dummy therapy or a dummy medication which (unknown to the participants) has no real effect.

Placebo group: a group of participants who are given a placebo. Groups given a therapy or medicine must improve more than the placebo group before the treatment can be considered to have any beneficial effect.

Population: a group to which the results of an investigation are intended to apply. Studies typically investigate smaller groups, called 'samples' drawn from the appropriate population. A population need not include every individual in a country; we can quite well speak of the population of ten-year-old girls, for example.

Probability: a number between 0 and 1 which expresses how likely it is that some event will occur. If the probability is near 0, the event is unlikely. If the probability is near 1, the event is almost certain to occur.

Qualitative: having to do with what kind something is. For example, red, blue and green lights are qualitatively different. Compare 'quantitative'.

Quantitative: having to do with how much there is of something. For example, bright and dim light are quantitatively different (bright light is more of the same thing). Compare 'qualitative'.

Questionnaire: a list of questions in written form, usually requiring fairly brief answers.

Quota sample: a type of sample obtained by selecting available individuals until a sufficient number (a quota) of each of a number of specified types has been obtained.

Random sample: a type of sample in which every member of the population has the same chance of being included.

Randomize: to arrange things, such as the sequence in which tasks are carried out, in an order determined by chance.

Ranks: numbers 1, 2, 3, and so on, often used in place of measurements that have been made on an ordinal scale. Ranks are allocated so that the smallest score gets the rank 1, the next is 2, and so on. If two or more scores are equal, all of them are given the average of the ranks they would have had if they had been slightly different from each other.

Ratio scale: a scale of measurement in which we know that equal differences between numbers indicate equal differences in the attribute that is measured, and also know that a numerical value of zero corresponds to the complete absence of the attribute. It is only if we have measured on a ratio scale that it is meaningful to speak about one score being, say, ten times as great as another.

Reactivity: a change in behaviour caused by the behaviour being observed or by the participant's expectations.

Relative quantitative term: an expression such as 'bigger' or 'faster' which describes the size or strength of something by comparing it to something else.

Representative sample: a sample intended to reflect the composition of the population.

Respondent: a person who answers questions.

Sample: a smaller group selected for study from a larger group, called a 'population', to which the results are intended to apply.

Self-selected sample: a sample where choices or actions by individuals in the population influence whether or not that individual is included in the sample. A self-selected sample is almost always a 'biased sample'.

Significance test: calculation of the probability of obtaining results such as those observed if the null hypothesis is true. If the probability is less than 0.05, the result is said to be 'significant' and we reject the null hypothesis as an adequate explanation for the results. When that happens, the alternative hypothesis that there is a real difference between groups is preferred to the null hypothesis that there is no such difference.

Significant: see 'Null Hypothesis' and 'significance test'.

Statistic: a numerical value calculated from data to represent some property of the data. For example, a mean, a range and a correlation coefficient are all statistics.

Statistical significance: refers to a result showing that the probability of obtaining results like those observed has a probability of occurring by chance that is small. By convention, results are usually regarded as statistically significant if the probability is less than 0.05 (1 in 20).

Statistical Table: a table showing the probability of obtaining results indicated by the size of a particular statistic.

Study: a broad term referring to any method of collecting data, such as experiments, surveys, interviews and so on (equivalent to 'investigation').

Subject (in an investigation): a person or animal whose actions or attributes form part of the results. The term 'participant' is usually preferred in the case of people.

Subjective: depending on the opinions or preferences of individuals. It is contrasted with 'objective'.

Survey: a method of data collection in which the attitudes, opinions or actions of a group are studied by asking questions.

Unfalsifiable: a term used to describe a model or hypothesis that no data can disprove. An unfalsifiable model or hypothesis is incapable of making firm predictions (since firm predictions can be disproved by data). Consequently it is practically valueless.

Variable: in an investigation, it is some feature that is capable of varying, whether it does vary or not. See also 'dependent variable' and 'independent variable'.

ANSWERS TO SELF-ASSESMENT QUESTIONS

SAQ 1 (a) The first conclusion is general because there are no exceptions to it. The second is aggregate, because it's only true of *most* ten- and eight-year-olds. There are eight-year-olds who know more words than some ten-year-olds.

(b) Possible conclusions of the opposite kind:
Adult rabbits have more offspring than adult mice. (*Aggregate*: some don't.) Ten-year-old children have had more birthdays than eight-year olds. (*General*: true of all of them if we ignore those born on 29 Feb!) Note that this isn't an interesting conclusion, and emphasises that almost all *psychological* conclusions are aggregate ones.

SAQ 2 If the result of an experiment does not agree with the prediction of a model, either because something happens that the model says must not happen or because something doesn't happen that the model says must happen, then the model *must be wrong*. It may not be *completely* mistaken, but it can not be entirely satisfactory either. At the very least, it must be incomplete. On the other hand, no matter how many times we obtain results that the model predicts, we have not proved that future predictions will also be upheld. We may not have tried to use the model in any of the situations where it does not work. For example, we might continue for ever proposing Ozzipandian house numbers in the same way, by adding 1 every time, and all of them would be legal, just as the model predicts, yet the model of adding one every time is not correct.

Even if we also collect many negative instances, we can not prove that a model is correct. Suppose our model is that every number in a street must be different, but the law is: *Any number that has not been used before, except prime numbers over 1000.* We might try thousands of numbers, all correctly predicted by our model to be acceptable or unacceptable without hitting on one of these rare exceptions which are, however, part of the law!

SAQ 3 Age and weight can each be measured on a *ratio* scale because the units are of constant size and we know what is meant by zero. As a result, it is meaningful to say that one person is half the age of another or that one weighs three times as much as another.

Mathematical ability is not a very precise concept – someone might be good at some kinds of maths and poor at others – so it would need to refer to performance on some particular test. It is very unlikely that we could be confident that the difference in ability between those scoring 10 and 20, say, is equivalent to the difference between those scoring 70 and 80, so the measurement is on an *ordinal* scale.

Vocabulary size and family size both appear to be measured by counting something. For family size, counting is indeed possible, as long as we define exactly which relatives are to be included, so it is measured on an *absolute* scale. (Though it would not be wrong to call it a *ratio* scale.) But for vocabulary, counting is not possible, partly because people know too many words to count them all, and partly because there is no clear boundary between known and unknown words. People usually have a vague idea of the meanings of lots of words they can't define exact-ly or use correctly. Therefore we would have to estimate vocabulary size by using a test containing both common and uncommon words. Those with larger vocabularies would obtain higher scores but measurement would be on an *ordinal* scale.

SAQ 4 (a)
Experiment
1. Nuisance variables are held constant.
2. Two (or more) different situations are brought about to see how the outcomes differ.
3. Requires an artificial situation that may not be representative of real life.
4. Can be repeated in every important detail.
5. Gives convincing evidence about cause and effect.

Observational study
1. Most nuisance variables cannot be controlled.
2. Nothing is done to affect what would otherwise occur.
3. The situation is natural and unaffected by the study so far as possible.
4. Can not be repeated in detail.
5. It is often uncertain which of two events causes the other, (or both may be caused by something else).

(b) Experiments and observational studies both record behaviour that occurs. Surveys record what people say or the choice of answer that they select.

SAQ 5 (a) Beliefs and attitudes are most easily ascertained by *surveys* carried out by means of questionnaires or interviews. We are very unlikely to see behaviour that is relevant to the question merely by *observing* at random. *Participant observation* in a group known to be interested in mysterious phenomena could yield information about that group, but not about the general population. It would be difficult to devise any ethical experiment, since an *experiment* on that topic would require some deception of participants.

(b) The most effective approach by far is an *experiment*. A *survey* is possible, asking people about their experience with each of the medicines, but there is a danger that the results would tell us more about public attitudes (doubtless affected by advertising and factors like the appearance of the medicines) than about their effectiveness. An observational study would be unlikely to yield a useful amount of data.

(c) An *observational study* would be easy to carry out and entirely appropriate. A *survey* would not be any easier to perform than an observational study and the results would depend on what people say rather than what they do, so it has no real merit. A *field experiment* can be useful if we want to focus particularly on things that do not happen very often, such as the way pedestrians pass someone who is pushing a pram, or a couple walking arm-in-arm. We arrange for assistants to behave in the required way and see how other members of the public act.

SAQ 6 The identification of which foods are inclined to be fattening is largely subjective. (All foods are fattening if you eat enough!) Different people may easily have different opinions on the matter. To minimize the problem, particular types of food should be listed and the shoppers could be asked which they have bought.

There is likely to be some reactivity in that people may feel defensive about buying food that they consider to be fattening. As a result, they may be reluctant to report some purchases if they are described as fattening. A possible improvement is not to mention whether or not the foods are thought to be fattening but only to ask which have been bought. We can discover people's opinions about which are considered fattening in a separate survey which does not involve asking people what they have bought. Another possibility is to ask the shoppers which foods they consider to be fattening only *after* they have reported which foods they have bought.

There is a sampling problem if shoppers in only one supermarket have been questioned. They are an *opportunity sample* and are likely not to be at all representative of the general population. For example, some supermarkets are used mainly by people with cars, others mainly by local pedestrians, and the types of food on sale can also vary from one store to another. To improve the study, several supermarkets of different types could be studied. Alternatively, the conclusions of the study can be restricted to apply only to shoppers in that particular supermarket. If a large proportion of those questioned refuse to answer, we also have a self-selected sample, with those who reply being perhaps rather different from the average.

SAQ 7   The quality of the photographs is again the dependent variable. The weather at the time the photographs were taken is the independent variable and all the others (such as Victoria's skill and the place where the photographs were taken) are nuisance variables. Even though Victoria says that in Crete the weather was always good, the independent variable is *not* the place where the photographs were taken. Probably some of her other pictures were *also* taken in good weather.